EXPLORING ENERGY
WIND AND WATER POWER

PHILIP SAUVAIN

Editorial planning
Deborah Tyler

M
MACMILLAN

First published 1987

Published by
MACMILLAN EDUCATION LTD
Houndmills, Basingstoke, Hampshire RG21 2XS
and London
Companies and representatives
throughout the world

Designed and produced by BLA Publishing Limited,
East Grinstead, Sussex, England.

Also in LONDON · HONG KONG · TAIPEI · SINGAPORE · NEW YORK

A Ling Kee Company

Illustrations by Fiona Fordyce, Tony Gibbons/Linden Artists, Sallie Alane Reason, Val Sangster/Linden Artists, Brian Watson/Linden Artists and BLA Publishing
Colour origination by Chris Willcock Reproductions
Printed in Hong Kong

British Library Cataloguing in Publication Data

Sauvain, Philip
    Exploring energy : wind and water power.
    — (Macmillan world library).
    1. Wind power — Juvenile literature
    2. Water-power — Juvenile literature
    I. Title
    621.4'5   TK541

ISBN 0-333-44175-3
ISBN 0-33-44180-X Series

Photographic credits

t = top b = bottom l = left r = right

cover: ZEFA; Chris Fairclough Picture Library

5 Alex Williams/Seaphot; 9 Frank Lane Picture Library; 10, 11, 12, ZEFA; 14 Mansell Collection; 15*t* ZEFA; 15*b* The National Trust; 17 ZEFA; 18*t* South American Pictures; 18*b*, 21*t* ZEFA; 21*b* South American Pictures; 22 Peter Stevenson/Seaphot; 23 British Columbian Embassy; 29*t* Chris Fairclough Picture Library; 29*b*, 31 ZEFA; 33 Central Electricity Generating Board; 34*t* Chris Fairclough Picture Library; 34*b* South American Pictures; 35 David Redfern/Seaphot; 36 South American Pictures; 37, 38 ZEFA; 39, 40 Science Photo Library; 41 Chris Fairclough Picture Library; 42 Frank Lane Picture Agency; 43 Japan Ship Company; 44*t*, 44*b* ZEFA

Note to the reader
In this book there are some words in the text which are printed in **bold** type. This shows that the word is listed in the glossary on page 46. The glossary gives a brief explanation of words which may be new to you.

Contents

Introduction

Energy gives us heat and light. It moves machines. It makes all things, even plants, streams, and the sea, grow or move. We cannot see or feel this energy but we can see the work it does. We need energy in order to live.

Energy is work

Scientists used a Greek word, 'energeia', which means 'work' when they first thought about what makes things move. The scientists changed the Greek word to 'energy'. Energy makes things move and do work. Work can also make other things move. Work makes heat, and heat can also make other things work. Energy always changes into some other type of energy when it is used.

You may think we can make energy, such as a power station which makes electricity. In fact, electricity is always made from some other types of energy. These include fast rivers, the wind, the waves, gas, oil and coal. The only kind of energy we make is our own personal energy. The food we eat gives us our energy.

▶ Windsurfers use the energy of both wind and water. When wind fills the sail, the board moves faster through the water.

▼ Wind and water power will provide the world with energy long after all the world's coal, oil and natural gas have been burned.

Uses of energy throughout the world

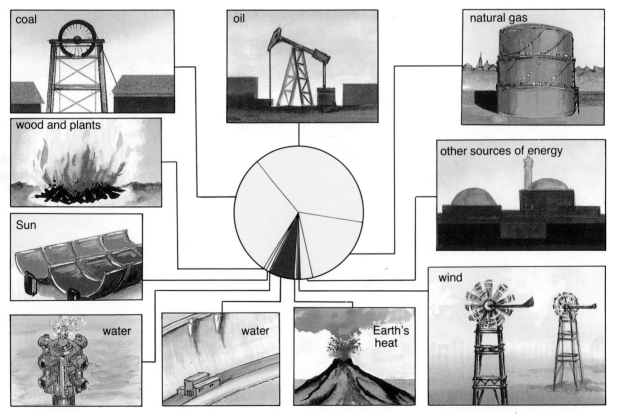

Types of energy

Scientists say there are two main types of energy. The first type of energy is stored in coal, in food, in lakes and rivers, or in the Sun. It is energy that is ready for use. We call it **potential energy**. We store potential energy when we eat a meal or fill the tank of a car with petrol. When this energy is being used, it is the second type of energy called **kinetic energy**. We use kinetic energy when we run or when a car moves. A river floats a boat down to the sea, or turns a water wheel. It is using kinetic energy.

Using energy

Some people use much more of the world's energy than others. They live in countries where there are many industries. They use energy to power machines in factories and hospitals and to light streets and buildings. They also use energy to heat homes and to move cars, trains and planes.

Different types of energy do different work. We use electricity to heat homes, light streetlights, and make machines work. **Electrical energy** is the most useful type of energy. It can be turned on with the flick of a switch. Some energy comes from **chemical** changes. The substances, or chemicals, in a battery make electricity so you can get light when you switch on a torch. Chemical energy also makes heat when we burn coal.

The power stored in the metal uranium produces **nuclear energy** in nuclear power stations. Some people use the Sun's rays to heat panels fixed to the roofs of their homes. These solar panels heat their water. This is called **solar energy**.

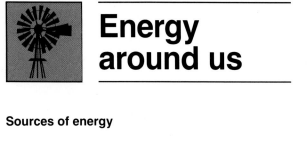

Energy
around us

oil

natural gas

The Sun supplies the Earth with all of its energy. Energy is all around us. It is stored in the things we see each day. The Sun's energy helps plants to grow. It makes rain. It causes winds. Lakes, rivers and the oceans store the Sun's energy as water. Trees store the Sun's energy as wood. Trees, plants and creatures stored some of the Sun's energy millions of years ago. Their remains rotted to form coal, oil and **natural gas**.

The Sun's heat

Over 5000 million years ago the Earth was a ball of liquid rock. Slowly, the surface of the Earth cooled. Today, there is still boiling liquid rock deep below the Earth's surface. This heat from the boiling liquid rock makes hot water under the ground. There is hot water in the springs at the Yellowstone National Park in the United States. Hot water from under the Earth's surface is used to heat buildings in New Zealand, Italy and Iceland. This heat from the Earth is called **geothermal energy**.

Winds and water

Energy from the Sun heats the land on the Earth during the day. The heat from the land warms the air above. Warm air rises because it is lighter than cold air. Cold air sinks. This is why the air above the hot lands at the **Equator** is always rising. Air from colder lands moves in to

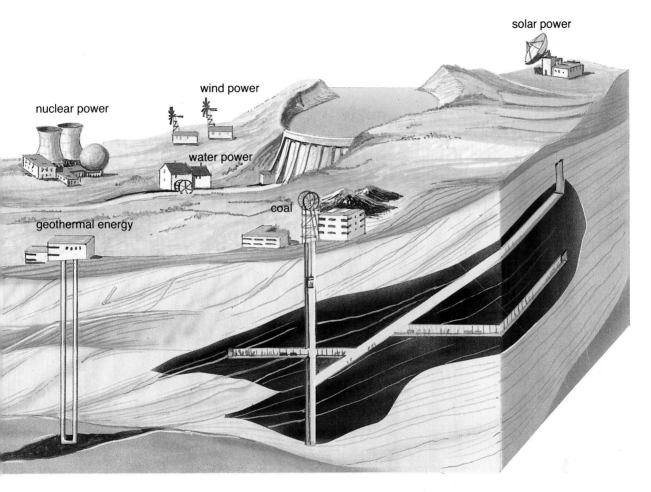

solar power

wind power

nuclear power

water power

geothermal energy

coal

take its place. This movement of air from cold to hot lands and from hot to cold lands produces **wind currents**.

The Sun also heats the surface of the Earth's oceans. Winds and the way the Earth turns keep the oceans moving. Some of the warmer water moves towards the cold seas. Colder water moves towards the warm seas. These movements of water are called **ocean currents**.

Weather

The Sun's heat turns water from the sea into tiny droplets in the air called **water vapour**. The vapour forms clouds. The same thing happens when a wet bathing costume dries in the Sun. The water in the costume turns to water vapour. It disappears into the air. The water **evaporates**. The water vapour in the clouds falls back to Earth in the form of rain. Rain falls into lakes and rivers and the water returns to the sea.

Using energy from wind and water

Wind and water have been used as sources of energy for thousands of years. People are now trying to find new ways of using wind power and water power. There are good reasons for this interest. There will always be winds. There will always be water. This is because they are replaced, or renewed, by the Sun. We call them **renewable** sources of energy.

Winds

The air around the Earth is called its **atmosphere**. It is divided into layers. The lower layer is called the **troposphere**. It is about 12 km in height. Our weather is formed there. In this layer the air is always moving. Gases in the upper layer of the atmosphere press down on the air in the lower layer. This weight is called **air pressure**.

Wind patterns

Warm air is lighter than cold air. Air pressure is lower at the Equator because the weather there is hot. Air pressure is higher at the North and South Poles because the weather there is cold. Cold air is heavier than warm air. These areas of **high pressure** and **low pressure** affect our weather. The warm air at the Equator rises into the higher levels of the troposphere.

Cooler air from the North and South Poles moves in to take its place. As the cooler air is heated up by the Sun, it also rises and more cool air moves in. The air in the troposphere is always kept moving. These movements cause winds. They blow in the same direction for much of the year. You can see these wind patterns on the map.

The direction of the wind depends mostly on the way the Earth turns. The turning movement of the Earth is called its **rotation**. Winds blowing south from the North Pole to the Equator swing around to the right because of the rotation of the Earth. If you live between the Tropic of Cancer and the Equator, the winds usually blow irom the north east. South east winds blow from the Tropic of Capricorn to the Equator. Sailors came to know these wind patterns. They called them the Trade Winds.

▼ Hot air rises. Then cold air takes its place. The cold air also heats up and rises. The flow of air continues to go around and around.

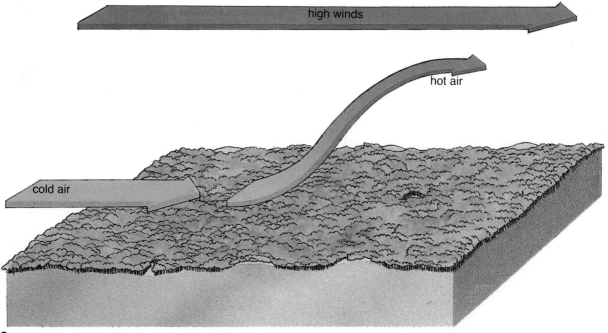

high winds

hot air

cold air

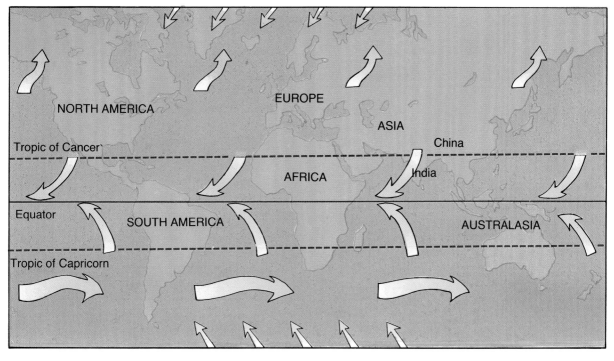

▲ Knowing about the winds was very important in the days of the sailing ship. Skilful use of the Trade Winds helped sailors to take goods to many different countries. Wool, tin and wood came from the northern countries. Silks and spices came from China and India.

▼ You can feel the power of the wind in a storm. The strongest winds are called hurricanes. A hurricane caused this damage to property in Houston in the United States.

The power of the wind

In the days before ships had engines, all large ships had sails. The ships used the power of the wind to take them from port to port. The first sea traders we know about were sailors from Egypt. About 12 000 years ago, they found out how to use the wind's power to push sailing boats. Later, the power of the Trade Winds was used to get goods to ports quickly.

People also found another way of using the wind when they built windmills. The wind's power moved the windmill's sails around, and made the **millstones** turn. Today we use wind power to make electricity. Using the wind as a source of power has many advantages. The wind is free. It is always there. It can be used during most days of the year.

Windmills

The first farmers worked very hard to grow food. They dug up the ground, sowed seeds and cut their crops. They grew cereals like wheat or corn. They rubbed the ears of corn between large flat stones called millstones to make flour. Some of the farmers used animals to pull ploughs or to carry heavy loads. Other people did all of their work by hand. They had no other source of power until the water wheel and the windmill were invented.

The first windmills

About 1300 years ago, the people of **Persia** in the Middle East began to use windmills. At first, the Persians used the windmills to lift water from rivers and wells. Later, the cloth sails were put inside buildings with long rooms. These rooms had narrow slits in the walls. When the wind blew through these slits in the walls, it turned the cloth sails.

▲ People on the Greek island of Crete saw how the wind moved their sailing boats. They worked out that similar sails on a windmill would turn a wheel. Today, there are still windmills with boat sails being used in southern Europe.

The sails were fixed to an upright, or **vertical**, pole. The end of this pole, or main **shaft**, turned a millstone on the floor above. The sails of this type of windmill turned around parallel with the floor, so they are called **horizontal mills**.

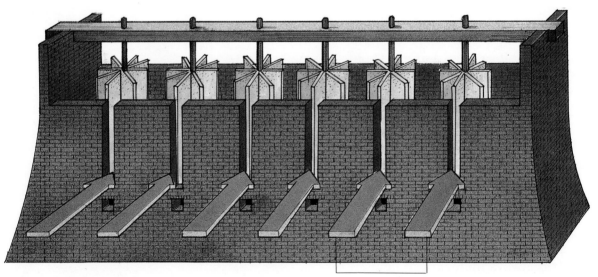

A horizontal windmill

wind

10

▲ This is the inside of an old wooden windmill. The heavy millstone on the right is turned by the gear wheel above it.

Windmills in Europe

About 800 years ago, people in Europe began to build wooden windmills. These windmills had long, narrow, canvas sails on the outside of the building. These sails turned at right angles to the ground instead of parallel with the ground. Windmills of this type are called **vertical mills**. The earliest vertical mill was called a **post mill**. The end of the main shaft was linked to wheels which turned the millstone. These mills were built on a thick central post, so that the miller could turn the whole of the post mill to face into the wind. This was very hard work. In 1745, in Britain, Edmund Lee invented the fantail. It was a set of small blades, or **vanes**. The blades were fitted to the main sails of the windmill at right angles. Millers were amazed to see that the fantail turned the windmill around by itself to face into the wind.

Taller windmills, called **tower mills** or **smock mills**, made good use of the fantail. They were first built about 500 years ago. Most of these mills were made of brick or stone. They were built on hills so they were able to use the stronger winds which blow higher above the ground. Only the cap of the tower mill, with its fantail and sails, turned around to face the wind.

Using windmills

People used windmills to grind corn, to crush seeds, to grind chalk, and to saw wood. Five hundred years ago, the Dutch people started to drain the flooded parts of their country. They used energy from windmills to help them with this work. Windmills helped to pump the water away from the land.

Water wheels

▼ The Asi River turns these huge water wheels at Hammah in Syria. The water wheels provide power for pumps which supply water to nearby houses.

People saw that running water had the power to move things. They felt this power when they waded through a river, or had to swim across it.

The Romans

The horizontal wheel was the simplest type of Roman water wheel. It had paddles fixed to a vertical shaft. These were spun around by a fast-flowing stream or river.

The shaft turned a grindstone in the building that was built above the stream.

The Romans also used vertical water wheels. A Roman engineer called Marcus Vitruvius Pollio wrote about these water wheels about 2000 years ago. This is why they are sometimes called Vitruvian wheels. The Romans may have seen these wheels first in some of the countries they conquered.

Types of water wheel

There are three main types of water wheel. When the water in a river pushes a wheel from below, the wheel is called an **undershot** wheel. The water shoots under the wheel. Undershot wheels suit slow rivers, such as those rivers found in flat lands near the sea.

Water shoots over the top of some wheels to make them spin. The **overshot** wheel works best in fast-flowing rivers. This is why they were often built in hilly areas where rivers ran downhill swiftly.

Wheels which turn when the water hits the blades in the middle of the wheel are called **breastshot** water wheels.

Water power was able to move all kinds of machinery. At first, water wheels were used to grind cereal crops. Later, they were used in forges to make iron and steel and in mills where cloth was made. By 1800, there were half a million water mills in Europe.

Bringing water to the mill

An overshot or breastshot water wheel had to have water flowing over it all the time in order to turn it. Narrow channels, called **aqueducts** or **leats**, took the water from the river to the water mill. The water flowed down a chute, called the **headrace**, to the water wheel. This flow was controlled by a special gate, called the **penstock**. Another channel, the **tailrace**, took the water back to the river after it had been used. In dry weather, the level of the rivers dropped. In order to keep the water flowing over the mill wheel, dams, or **weirs**, were built across the river. The water formed a mill pond behind the dam. The water in the pond was used when it was needed.

▼ In undershot wheels, the blades dip into the flowing water. In overshot wheels, the water falls on to the blade. Falling and flowing water turn the breastshot wheel.

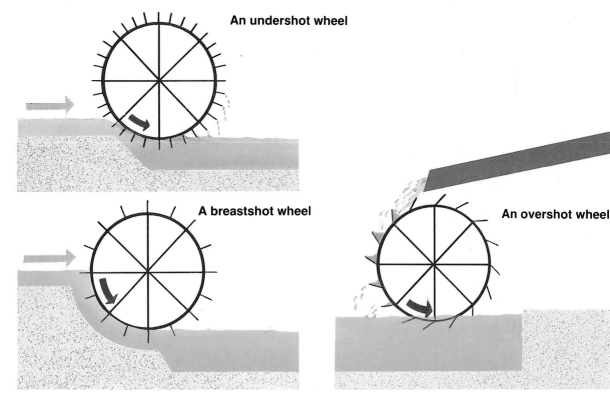

An undershot wheel

A breastshot wheel

An overshot wheel

Water wheels for industry

The first people on Earth lived in groups. They made their own shelters and grew their own food. They made their tools. They were skilled at many jobs.

The first machines

About 6000 years ago, the workers in the first towns began to develop special skills. Some people made pots. Other people spun thread or wove cloth. These were the first industries. Much later on, they used their hands or feet to work simple machines, such as the spinning wheel.

Water mills

Millers were probably the first people to use water power to work machines. They used them to turn the millstones which ground corn into flour. About 500 years ago, water wheels were used to crush chalk and rocks. Water wheels were also used to work machinery which squeezed oil out of olives. Woollen cloth could be cleaned by water power. The power came from the shaft of the water wheel as it turned. Blacksmiths used water power to lift their heavy hammers. When iron was hammered, it could be made into all kinds of tools.

People and animals get tired when they do heavy work. A water wheel does not.

▼ One mill can work for many people. Here, farmers are bringing sacks of grain to the water mill. The huge wheels under the mill turn the millstones.

▲ Water mills made it easier to do many jobs. An overshot wheel powers this 150 year old sawmill in the forests of New Brunswick, Canada. The power of the water helps to cut the wood.

The water wheel goes on working as long as there is water to turn the wheel. Richard Arkwright used a water wheel to power the world's first cotton-spinning mill in Britain in 1771. Soon many other cloth-makers built spinning mills with water wheels in river valleys.

Mills and rivers

Water power was cheap but it did have problems. Water wheels worked slowly. They could turn only a few machines at the same time. In dry weather, the level of the water in the pond dropped. Mud choked up the mill pond. Weeds grew in the mud. The mill pond and the mill stream had to be cleaned out from time to time.

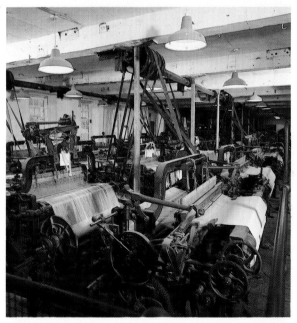

▲ The power for these weaving machines comes from a huge water wheel. The wheel turns the iron shaft on the roof. The belts take power to the weaving machines.

Falling water

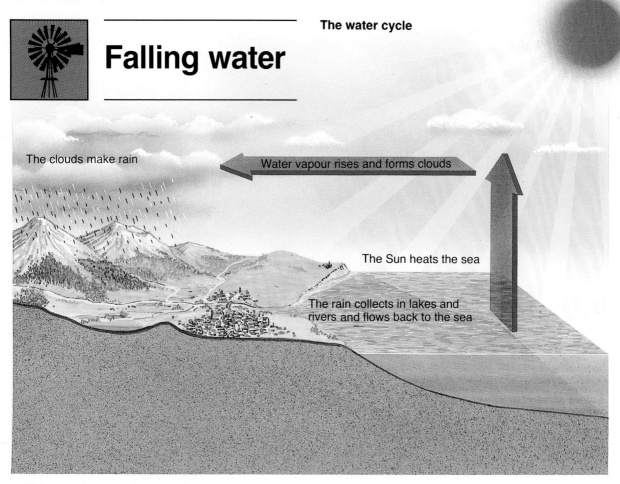

The clouds make rain

Water vapour rises and forms clouds

The Sun heats the sea

The rain collects in lakes and rivers and flows back to the sea

When a ball is thrown into the air, it falls back to the ground. It does not go on and on up into the sky. The power which pulls the ball back to Earth is called the **force of gravity**. Gravity pulls everything downwards, including rain, rivers and falling water.

Moving water

Water is always on the move. It goes around and around in a circle called the **water cycle**. The cycle begins when the Sun heats the sea. Heat causes water vapour to rise up into the air. Hot air can take up a lot more water vapour than cold air. This is why wet things, like clothes, dry quickly on hot days.

The water vapour forms clouds. These clouds cool when they rise over hills or pass over land. When the clouds get colder, they are unable to hold all their water. The force of gravity makes the water in the clouds fall as rain, hail, or snow.

The rain runs into pools and small streams. The pools and streams run into bigger rivers and lakes. Sea level is almost always lower than land level, so the force of gravity makes the water flow towards the sea again.

This is how clouds, rain and rivers store energy from the Sun. The Sun's energy lifts the water from the seas and puts it into lakes and rivers. Today, we use the energy in falling water to produce electricity. We call this a **hydro-electric power** system. The word 'hydro' comes from a Greek word, 'hydor', for water.

Waterfalls

Have you ever watched a waterfall? If you have, you know how powerful a waterfall is. The energy is in the water all the time. Engineers have found out how to use water to make energy when we most need it. They build dams above waterfalls to keep back the water. This makes a lake, or **reservoir**, of the water. From there, the water flows down to a lower level through pipes. The pipes can be opened and closed. The energy in the flowing water is turned into electricity. We can choose when to make the electricity. We make electricity when we need it, because we cannot store it. We can only store the water.

▶ You can see the power of falling water in this waterfall in Wyoming in the United States. The water has made a deep hole at the bottom of the Yellowstone Falls. The strong flow of water has cut a steep-sided valley through the rock.

Building dams

A dam stops water from flowing. The level of the water rises and spreads out behind the dam, where it forms a reservoir. The weight of this water presses against the dam wall. Engineers have to make sure the dam will be strong enough to stand up against this pressure. Water pouring down the valley from a broken dam can destroy everything in its path. It can also drown people and animals.

Finding a place to build a dam

Engineers search hard for a good place to build a dam. They look for a river which will keep the dam filled up with water, even in dry weather. They look for a deep, narrow valley where the river falls steeply. There is more power in water which falls steeply. The height from which the water falls to the power station is called the **head of water**. Also, engineers need less earth, rocks and concrete to build a dam across a narrow valley. Dams are very expensive to build.

▲ The Paraná River forms the border between Brazil and Paraguay in South America. The land is flat but both countries needed electricity. In 1975, they began to build the Itaipu Dam.

◄ The Itaipu Dam is nearly finished here. A large area behind the dam has been flooded to make a reservoir. Water is flowing down the spillway. The dam has enough head of water to provide Paraguay and Brazil with electricity.

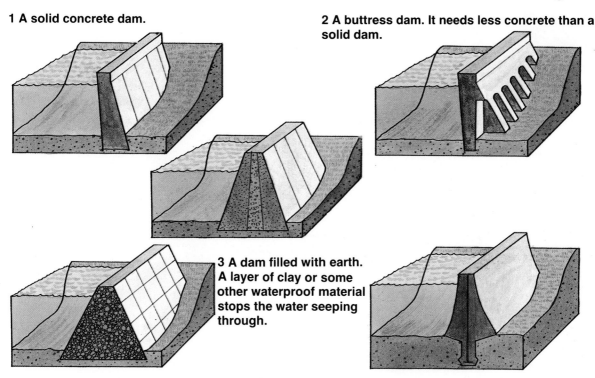

1 A solid concrete dam.

2 A buttress dam. It needs less concrete than a solid dam.

3 A dam filled with earth. A layer of clay or some other waterproof material stops the water seeping through.

4 A dam filled with rocks or stones. It is lined with concrete or steel plates.

5 A dam with deep foundations made of steel.

Types of dam

The type of dam chosen for a valley depends partly on the rocks and earth found nearby. These rocks and earth may be used as building materials. Some dams are made of thick, solid concrete all the way across. These dams hold back the water just because they are so heavy. They slope backwards at an angle.

Buttress dams also slope backwards at an angle. They have huge, solid concrete supports at the front. These buttresses strengthen the dam wall.

Many of the world's largest dams are made either out of earth or rocks and stones. Dams filled with rocks and stones have a smooth outer surface, or skin, made out of sheets of concrete or steel plating. Engineers strengthen some dams by sinking strong steel supports deep into the rocks below the ground.

Sometimes there is too much water in the reservoir. A **spillway** is built to let the water drain away and take the pressure off the dam.

Changes in the countryside

Building a dam always changes the countryside. New roads are built. Trucks use the roads to bring machinery and materials to build the dam. Sometimes a road runs right across the dam wall.

Dams are often built in places which are far away from towns or villages. So the workers who build the dams need somewhere to live. Houses or hotels are built for them. When a reservoir is formed behind a newly-built dam, the water floods farms and homes. If people live in the valley where a dam is to be built, they are moved to other areas. Life in the valley is changed completely.

The need for more power

At the beginning of the 1800s, the first factory owners soon found they had to have more power. They knew that the more goods they made, the more they would sell. A single water wheel could only power a few machines. So the factory owners looked for ways of making extra power to drive more machines. Some people began to use a new type of water wheel called a **turbine**.

A water turbine

Water turbines

Benoit Fourneyron invented the water turbine in France in 1827. He made falling water swirl around as it rushed down a pipe. The force of this spinning water turned the blades on a wheel.

Many factories in Europe, Mexico and South America first used these turbines about 150 years ago.

The water turbine made it possible to make hydro-electricity from running water. Water passes through an opening in the dam wall controlled by **sluice gates**. It falls steeply down tubes to the shaft which feeds water to the turbine. The force of the water makes the turbine spin rapidly. The turbine drives a machine which makes electricity.

◀ Wind turbines are still an unusual sight in the countryside. They can be used to make electricity for people's homes.

Wind turbines

The windmill was a simple type of turbine. It moved something like a turbine in slow motion. Today, wind generators spin very rapidly indeed. They have streamlined vanes, blades or propellers. Wind generators like these only work when the wind speed is at least 16 km an hour.

There are two main types of wind turbine. Vertical turbines with a horizontal shaft have two or three blades. They spin very fast like the propellers on a plane. Horizontal wind turbines look like giant eggbeaters. They spin around on an upright shaft. The turbines can use the wind when it blows from any direction.

▶ Inside the power house beneath the Itaipu Dam. The water turbines began to generate electricity in 1985. They will work at full power in 1990.

Water power

Falling water turns turbines which make, or **generate**, electricity from water power. Hydro-electricity power systems make about a quarter of the world's electricity. They use a renewable source of energy. Rain fills up the lakes and rivers again with water which supplies the power.

Water from the mountains

Many hydro-electric power systems are built in the hills or mountains where there are waterfalls and fast-flowing rivers.

Heavy rainfall keeps the rivers filled with water. The main disadvantage is that few people live in the mountains. Most of the world's hydro-electricity is taken to distant towns and factories. Tasmania makes one-tenth of the electricity Australia uses. Yet only one-twentieth of the people of Australia live in Tasmania. Some hydro-electricity systems, however, have brought new industries to new towns built in the mountains.

▼ The Spokane River in the United States is a good site for hydro-electric power. The narrow dam is built against the rock of the valley sides. Water flows down the pipes at the sides into the power house. The rate of flow of the river is controlled over the spillway.

▲ The Kitimat Project in Canada.

The Kitimat Project

Kitimat today is a city of over 10000 people. Before the hydro-electric system was built, only a few trappers and hunters lived in the area. A company which makes aluminium built the system and the town. They needed cheap electricity to make the aluminium.

Engineers first built a huge dam across the Nechako River. This was the Kenney Dam. It was built on a site about 250 km from Kitimat. The dam formed a huge reservoir. The water in the dam falls 800 km through a tunnel in Mount DuBose. Engineers built the Kemano Power Station inside the mountain. The mountain helps to withstand the force of the falling water. The water turns the turbines which make electricity.

Tall steel towers, called **pylons**, carry cables which take the electricity from Kemano to Kitimat. These cables are called **power lines**. They cross the lonely Kildala Pass. This is why the project is sometimes called the 'Four K project': Kenney, Kemano, Kildala and Kitimat.

Hydro-electric systems

Hydro-electric power systems have been built all over the world. Most of them take their power from dams across rivers. Some systems are tiny. Others are huge. The Grande Dixence Dam in Switzerland is only 700 m long but it is nearly 300 m high. The Kiev Dam in the USSR is only 20 m high but it is over 50 km in length.

The biggest hydro-electric system in the world will soon be the earth-filled dam at Itaipu. This is on the Paraná River between Brazil and Paraquay in South America. Itaipu will produce six times as much electricity as a large power station buring coal.

▶ The orange areas of the map show which parts of the world produce the most hydro-electricity. In these areas, there are high mountains and long rivers. The chart shows how much hydro-electricity some countries use. The United States uses more hydro-electricity than any other country.

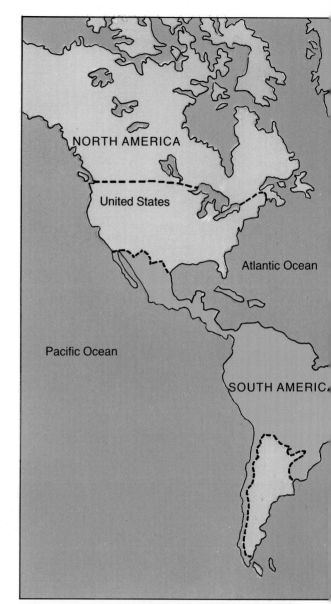

The highest, biggest, longest dams in the world			
	Name of dam	*Country*	*Measurements*	*Type*
Tallest dams	Rogun	USSR	335 m high	rock
	Nourek	USSR	317 m high	rock
	Grande Dixence	Switzerland	285 m high	concrete
Largest dams	Tarbela	Pakistan	142 million cubic m	earth
	Fort Peck	USA	96 million cubic m	earth

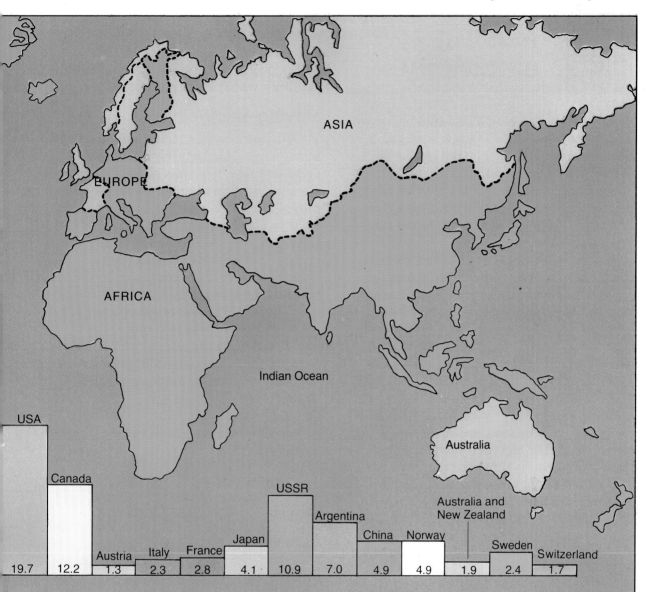

USA	Canada	Austria	Italy	France	Japan	USSR	Argentina	China	Norway	Australia and New Zealand	Sweden	Switzerland
19.7	12.2	1.3	2.3	2.8	4.1	10.9	7.0	4.9	4.9	1.9	2.4	1.7

The highest, biggest, longest dams in the world				
	Name of dam	Country	Measurements	Type
Longest dam	Yacryeta-Apipe	Argentina and Paraguay	72 km	earth
Largest reservoirs	Bratsk	USSR	169 cubic km of water	earth
	Aswan High Dam	Egypt	164 cubic km of water	earth
	Kariba	Zimbabwe	160 cubic km of water	concrete
	Akosombo	Ghana	148 cubic km of water	rock

Making electricity

Electricity was new a hundred years ago. Until that time, people knew something about electricity but they did not know what work it could do. Electricity has many advantages over other sources of energy. It is clean. It is always ready for use. It can also be made from **fossil fuels** such as oil and coal.

Fossil fuels cannot be renewed. Wind and water are renewable. This is why people have started to look again at wind and water power. We need the electricity which wind and water power can generate.

Making electricity yourself

You make electricity yourself. You have seen your hair stand on end after you pulled a jumper over your head. You may have rubbed a balloon and made it stick to the ceiling. The electricity which does this does not move. It remains still. This is why it is called **static electricity**.

Scientists have found out why static electricity behaves in this way. They now know that all things on Earth are made up of tiny atoms, about one ten-millionth of a millimetre in width. Each of these atoms contains even tinier bits, or particles, of electricity. There are two kinds of particle. They are **electrons** and **protons**. Atoms hold equal numbers of these particles. The electrons each have one type of electric force. We call it a negative electric charge.

The protons have a different force. It is a positive electric charge. An object with a negative charge is attracted to an object with a positive charge. It is repelled by anything which has a negative charge.

Moving electricity

Electrons can be made to move down a metal wire. The metal attracts, or **conducts**, the electrons along the wire. This is called an **electric current** because it moves like the current in a stream. In 1820, a Danish scientist called Hans Christian Oersted found out that an electric current could make an object attract other objects towards it. It could produce **magnetism**. Scientists then tried to find out if a magnet could produce electricity. Michael Faraday showed them that it could. He pushed a magnet into a coil of wire and out again. By doing this over and over again, Faraday made an electric current pass down the wire. Later on, this discovery made it possible to use water power and wind power to make electricity.

▶ Rubbing a balloon takes away some of its positive electric charges. This is why the negative charges in the balloon stick to the positive charges on the ceiling.

▼ The ancient Greeks were the first to know about static electricity. When they rubbed a stone called amber with silk, they found out that the stone could pick up pieces of dust and straw.

▼ A British scientist called William Gilbert used 'elektron', a Greek word for amber, when he invented the word 'electric' about 400 years ago. He used it to describe the way in which objects could be attracted to another object, such as iron filings to a magnet.

▲ In 1831, a British scientist called Michael Faraday showed that a magnet could produce electricity.

▲ In 1881, an American inventor called Thomas Alva Edison built an electricity generating station. It supplied electric power to people in the city of New York. This was the world's first public electricity service.

The big power stations

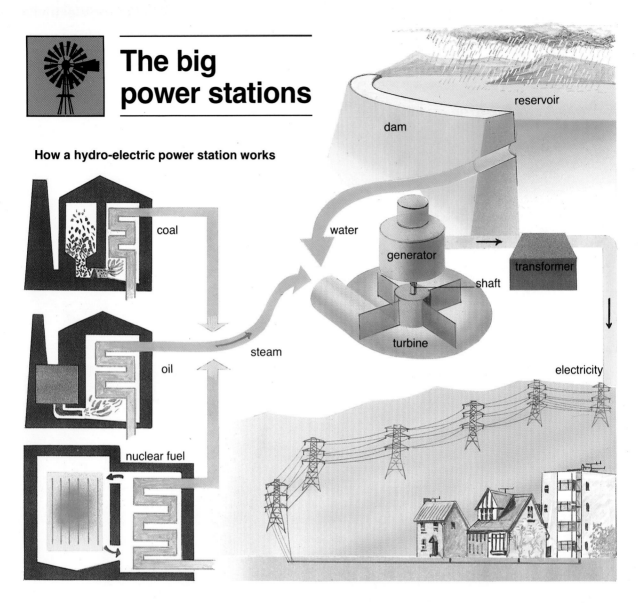

How a hydro-electric power station works

- reservoir
- dam
- coal
- water
- generator
- transformer
- shaft
- oil
- turbine
- steam
- electricity
- nuclear fuel

Faraday's method of making electricity is still used in power stations today. When the turbines spin around at high speed, they turn an electromagnet inside a coil of wire. The movement generates an electric current. This is why it is called a **generator**.

Water turbines are worked by water power in hydro-electric power systems. Other power stations burn fossil fuels, such as coal or oil, to make steam. The steam is then forced through a turbine. The steam spins the turbine blades. Nuclear power stations use the power in atoms to make electricity. This is called nuclear energy. The nuclear energy makes heat. The heat makes steam. The steam turns the turbine.

The electricity produced by these power stations is changed or transformed so that it can be sent along the power lines. A **transformer** makes the change. Sometimes the power lines are put underground, so that they do not spoil the countryside. The electricity is carried to offices, hospitals, factories and homes. It is used for heating, lighting and to work machines.

► The control room in a power station is worked by computers and automatic machines. Only a small number of people are needed to work in a power station.

► This dam is part of the Nurek hydro-electric scheme in the USSR. Fast-flowing water turns the turbines which make the electricity. Power lines carry the electricity away.

Supply and demand

Electricity is needed day and night throughout the year. The demand for electricity goes up each year. Schools, homes, hospitals, factories and farms all make use of electricity in thousands of different ways. Electricity is easy to use but it cannot be stored for future use. You cannot buy it and store it before you use it, like coal or oil. People use much more electricity at some times than at others. Power stations have to be able to supply electricity whenever people demand it.

Supply

Power stations supply electricity by sending it along the power lines. The power lines are often linked together to form a power grid. The grid supplies power to a large number of homes and buildings.

► Power lines are like rivers of electricity. They criss cross the country to take power to homes and factories. Many people think they spoil the countryside.

▼ In some parts of the world, the highest demand for electricity often occurs when a popular television programme comes to an end on a cold winter's night. At the same time, people in millions of homes switch on electric kettles or coffee machines to make a hot drink.

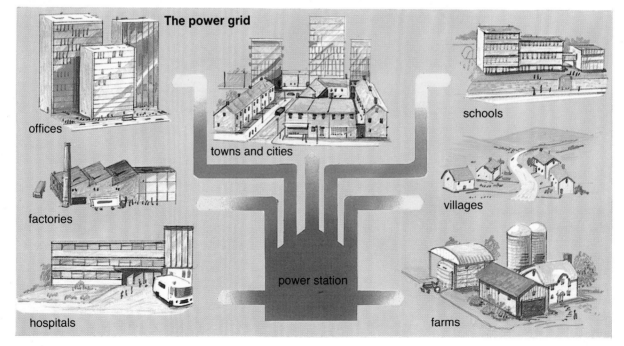

The power grid

offices

towns and cities

schools

factories

villages

hospitals

power station

farms

The flow of electricity is measured in **volts**. This is like measuring the flow of water in a large river. The turbines in most power stations generate electricity at a pressure of about 25 000 volts before the electricity is sent along the power lines. The pressure is then lowered so that it can be used safely in homes and factories. Homes, schools, shops and offices use electricity at a lower pressure than factories. Factories with large, powerful machines need electricity at a higher pressure.

Demand

People do not need the same amount of electricity all the time. Their demand varies. It depends on where they are and what they are doing. Demand for electricity is usually at its highest in the early evening during the winter. That is the time when many people come home from school and work. They turn on the lights and the heating, and they may start to cook a meal.

They may turn on the television. They will need electricity for some or all of these things. Much less electricity will be needed on a warm day in the summer.

The lowest amount of electricity needed every day throughout the year is called the **base load**. The greatest amount of electricity needed at special times is called the **peak load**.

Coal, oil and nuclear power stations generate electricity from steam. They make it cheaply when the turbines are running at top speed. It takes about eight hours to make the steam and start the turbines again if they have not been used for some time. This makes it hard to meet the demand for power if the weather suddenly turns very cold.

Hydro-electric power stations are easier to control. The water is always there. These stations can make electricity within two minutes of starting up. They can increase the supply of electricity very quickly.

Storing energy

Oil can be stored in a tank until it is needed. We cannot do this with wind power or electricity. We have to change them into another type of energy which we can store.

Wind power

Windmills can be used to make electricity from wind power. They make the most electricity on very windy days. Engineers use the extra electricity made on windy days to pump water from a lake up to a higher lake. On calm days, the wind generator shuts down. Then the water in the higher lake is allowed to fall to the lower level. The power of the falling water is used to make hydro-electricity. Wind generators can help to supply towns with electricity throughout the year.

Engineers can also use the extra electricity made on windy days to force, or compress, air into a tank. This **compressed air** can be stored until it is needed. It can be used on calm days to spin a turbine to generate electricity.

Using a wind generator to pump water

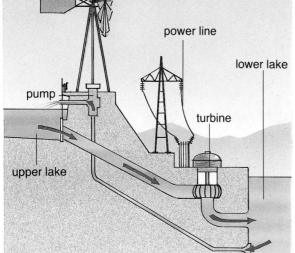

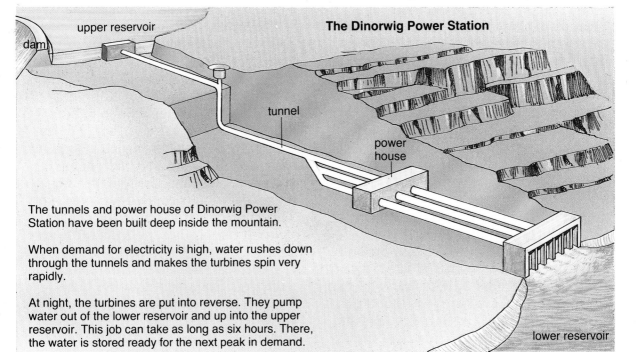

The Dinorwig Power Station

The tunnels and power house of Dinorwig Power Station have been built deep inside the mountain.

When demand for electricity is high, water rushes down through the tunnels and makes the turbines spin very rapidly.

At night, the turbines are put into reverse. They pump water out of the lower reservoir and up into the upper reservoir. This job can take as long as six hours. There, the water is stored ready for the next peak in demand.

▲ Dinorwig Power Station in North Wales. When the power station was designed, a great effort was made not to spoil the countryside. The power station is hidden from view. The upper reservoir is on the left of the picture. Can you see where the water enters the lower reservoir?

Water power

In some hydro-electric power systems, engineers use electricity to pump water up to a high reservoir late at night. This is when the demand for electricity is at its lowest. When the demand is high, the pumped water is brought down tubes to the power station to turn the turbines. This is called a **pumped storage system**. The biggest system of this type in Europe is at Dinorwig in North Wales. It is built in the mountains of Snowdonia.

The hydro-electric power stations which use the force of the Niagara River in the United States and Canada also use this method. At night, water is pumped up into the reservoir above the Robert Moses Power Station. The same thing happens at the Sir Adam Beck Power Station, on the Canadian side of the river. Both power stations use the river water to generate electricity during the peak periods during the day.

Using river power

The world's rivers release a huge amount of power in the form of kinetic energy as they flow back to the sea. So far, only a small part of this energy is used to produce power that we can use.

Small systems

Many countries have long, fast-flowing rivers passing through them. These rivers contain so much energy, they could be used over and over again to make electricity. Much of this water power could be used if small power stations were built along the river. Electricity can be generated even if the water level drops by only one metre. The author Rudyard Kipling used a small stream in his garden in Britain to make hydro-electricity over 80 years ago. He used the hydro-electric power to light his home. The people of China have built 90 000 small power stations along the rivers. This provides much of the electricity that China needs. Small power stations are often cheap to build and cheap to run.

▲ Farmers in South East Asia often use rivers to flood their fields on purpose. These farmers are planting rice seedlings in the water of the paddy fields.

▼ These water mills are anchored in the Danube River in Yugoslavia. The current of the river turns the wheels.

Floods

The energy and power of a big river can be seen when it floods. Floods often cause damage but they can be helpful as well. The Nile River used to flood its banks each year. It left rich mud on the banks when the water went down. The farmers of Egypt used the flood water for their crops. This is called **irrigation**. Now the Aswan High Dam controls the Nile River. The dam provides water for Egypt and its neighbour, Sudan.

Dams to hold back flood water have been built along the Tennessee River and its side valleys in the United States. The water is used to produce hydro-electricity and also for irrigation. If it is controlled, the power of a flooding river can benefit rather than harm the people who live along its valley.

▼ You can see how much energy there is in a river. Flooding can cause enormous damage. When rivers break their banks, they often wash away trees, roads, bridges and buildings.

Using the tides

The place where the river empties into the sea is called its **estuary**. Most river estuaries are tidal. Salt water in the sea moves up the river at high tide. About six hours later, at low tide, the salt water flows back into the sea.

Tides

The pull of the Sun and Moon causes the movement of the tides. In some places, the difference in height between high and low tide is only about a metre. It depends on the shape of the coast and on the ocean currents. The greatest difference in the rise and fall of the tide can be seen at the Bay of Fundy in Nova Scotia, Canada. The difference in height there is over 15 m.

Tide mills

Tides are a source of energy. People in northern France used tidal mills with water wheels over 900 years ago. Today, engineers are looking at new ways of using tidal power.

The machinery used in the old tidal mills was like that of a water mill. At high tide, the incoming sea water went through sluice gates into a mill pond. The sluice gates shut tight when the tide turned and the level of the water started to drop. The pond was then much higher than the level of the rest of the water in the estuary. The miller released the sea water from the pond at low tide. As the water rushed back to the sea from the pond, it turned a water wheel which was used to grind corn.

◄ Four hundred years ago, there were tide mills along the estuaries of many rivers in Britain and France. This picture shows the tidal mill at Woodbridge in England, at low tide.

▶ The dam across the Rance River in Brittany, France. Its 24 turbines are turned one way by the incoming tide. A few hours later, they are turned the other way by the outgoing tide.

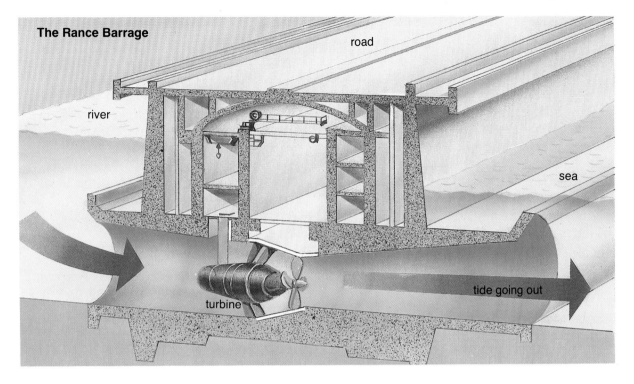

The Rance Barrage

road

river

sea

tide going out

turbine

Tidal power stations

Tidal power stations are in use in France and in the USSR. The Rance **Barrage** in France was built over 20 years ago. It uses the tides of the Rance River estuary to make electricity. At high tide, the river level is eight metres above the level at low tide. As the level rises, the water turns the turbines in the Rance power station. When the tide goes out, the water turns the turbines the other way. The power station makes enough electricity to supply an area the size of a large city. Why are there not more tidal power stations? The water power does exist. A huge tidal wave, called the 'Severn Bore' enters the Severn River estuary in Britain. Experts say it could make 30 times as much electricity as the Rance power station. The main problem is that tidal power stations are difficult and cost a lot to build. A plan to build a tidal power station in the Bay of Fundy in Canada failed. The cost of building a dam there was too expensive. Extra-strong dam walls would have been needed because the tides are so strong. Tidal power stations have other disadvantages. They can only produce electricity for a few hours each day. Half of this power is produced at night when there is little need for extra electricity.

Wave power

Nearly three-quarters of the Earth's surface is covered by water. Most of this is salt water. Scientists think it could provide us with energy in the future. This is because the surface of the ocean is rarely still. Currents move large quantities of water from one part of the ocean to another. Waves up to 25 m in height are formed. The force of these waves could become a valuable source of energy, if we knew how to control the force.

The power of the waves

Waves are formed by the wind. The strongest winds are those which blow over long stretches of sea or ocean. The strongest winds form crests of waves which are called **swells**. The longer and stronger the wind blows, the bigger the waves. Power made with these waves would help to meet the peak demand for electricity. This is because strong winds often bring bad weather. People use more electricity when the weather is bad.

▼ Waves damage the coast. They cut caves in cliffs and wash away beaches. Sometimes they destroy harbours and piers.

▲ Sea clams convert the energy of waves into electricity. They could be used to provide power for people on remote islands.

Using the waves

Engineers have invented many methods for using wave power, but not many have yet been tried out. Scientists are still working on them. Professor Stephen Salter at Edinburgh University has invented one method. It uses machines which float on the sea. The machine has flaps which are joined to a long central column, or shaft. The flaps move up and down as the waves pass them. They move a turbine which makes electricity. The flaps look like bobbing ducks, so the method is called the Salter Ducks.

Another method was invented by Sir Christopher Cockerell. The Cockerell Rafts are hinged in the middle. They flap up and down with the waves and force water through pumps.

A third method would use huge plastic bags. The waves would squash the air in the bags, and the air would drive a turbine. All these machines would be anchored in the seabed. They would have to be very strong to withstand the force of the sea.

Scientists in Norway have been working on two other methods for using wave power. The first wave power station was opened in Norway in 1985. Engineers built a tower, or column, in the sea cliffs near Bergen. The column is 20 m high and it is hollow. Waves rush in and out of the column. They push air in the tower upwards. The air falls back as the water flows out of the column. As the air moves up and down, it turns a special turbine. This method is called the Oscillating Water Column.

The second method is called Tapchan. Waves flow fast along a narrow concrete channel in the cliffs. They spill over into a reservoir. From there, the water flows through pipes to power a turbine.

Both of these methods were built with the help of the Salter team. They are cheaper ways of making electricity than some power stations which use coal and nuclear energy.

Many other methods are being designed, but these are the only two which have been built.

Using the wind

There is a new interest in windmills. This is because most people know that the world's fossil fuels, such as coal, oil and natural gas, will run out. As they become scarce, the price of fuel will rise. Wind, like water in the sea, is free. It will not run out.

Windpumps

Sixty years ago, there were over five million windpumps on the farms of the American West. Many are still in use today

◀ Howards's Knob windmill in North Carolina. The old windmills with their big sails have given way to vertical windmills or wind generators like this. They use huge propellers, like those on an aeroplane, with either two or three huge blades.

▶ Wind farms have to be built in places where there are good wind speeds and plenty of space. This wind farm is at Altamount in California in the United States.

for pumping water. The windpumps are metal towers which stand over a well. At the top of the towers are metal wheels. Each wheel has about 20 blades. When the wind blows, the wheels spin around, lifting water from the well into a storage tank. The water is used for crops and animals, as well as by the household.

In the 1930s, many wind generators were also built in North America. They made enough electricity to supply a single farm. They were simple to use and seldom went wrong. Wind generators are used in many parts of the world where a small, local supply of electricity is needed.

The world's largest windmill

In 1979, the world's largest windmill was built at Howard's Knob in North Carolina, in the United States. It has blades instead of sails. The blades are 60 m in length. This windmill generates enough electricity to supply about 500 homes. About 1000 similar windmills would be needed to take the place of a single power station burning coal or oil. One thousand giant windmills would take up a lot of space.

Wind farms

When groups of wind generators are built close to eah other we call them a 'wind farm'. Wind farms have been built to provide electricity in California in the United States. A similar wind farm is planned for the Isle of Man in the United Kingdom. Wind farms have to be built in places where it is very windy. This is not always close to the place where most people live, so electricity has to be carried to the towns. High towers are needed to make the best use of the winds. Giant wind generators can be dangerous. Blades can snap off in a gale. They are also very noisy. There is a constant whirring and swishing from the huge blades. Very few people would want to live close to a wind farm.

Building wind farms out at sea could be the answer. There are no hills, buildings or trees there to stop the wind reaching the generators. The noise of the whirring blades would not annoy anyone, although the towers would spoil the look of the sea. They might also be dangerous to ships at night or in a fog. They might also affect such wildlife as birds and fish.

Changing energy

Energy cannot be made or destroyed. It can be changed from one form to another, or moved from one place to another. For thousands of years, different ways of changing and using the Sun's energy have been tried. People have wanted to change energy to make their lives easier.

Food and animals

Our own energy comes from the food we eat. It is one of the main ways in which we make use of the Sun's energy. Sunlight helps plants to grow. The plants store the Sun's energy. They make a substance called **carbohydrate**. This is why carbohydrate is found in many of the foods we eat, such as cereals. It is a good source of energy for people too.

Carbohydrate is also found in food for animals. Stored energy passes from plants to animals when horses eat oats or barley. The horses store this energy for future use, so that it can be used to move their muscles. They change the stored energy in food into **mechanical energy** when they use their muscles to pull a cart or plough.

The horse was the main source of power before the steam engine. This is why energy was once measured in **horsepower**. A ten horsepower car did as much work as ten horses.

▼ Horses were more common than tractors on Europe's farms until about 1950. Cattle, horses, camels, llamas and other animals still do much of the hard work on some of the world's farms. Some of the stored energy in this crop is being eaten by the horse so he will have enough energy to pull the heavy cart.

Energy from wind and water

We also change energy from one form to another at a hydro-electric power station. The kinetic energy of moving water turns the water turbines to make electrical energy.

Sails change the kinetic energy of the wind into mechanical energy when a sailing boat moves through the water. Sailing ships sometimes took 100 days to cross the Atlantic Ocean from Europe to North America. Later, steam ships made the same journey in less than four days, but only after burning a large amount of fuel. It took about 1500 tonnes of fuel to make the return journey across the Atlantic Ocean. In future, we may see many more ships with sails as well as engines.

Heat from the sea

Energy has also been changed from one form to another in the Ocean Thermal Energy Converters (OTEC). The OTEC system has been tested in warm tropical seas. The system has been built to make use of the difference in heat between the surface of the sea and the water 30 m below the surface. This difference can be as much as 15°C to 20°C.

An Ocean Thermal Energy Converter

warm water

warm water

control centre

generator

cold water

cold water

OTECs use the energy in the warm water at the ocean surface to boil a liquid, such as ammonia. This liquid has a much lower boiling point than water. The gas given off by the boiling ammonia drives a turbine which makes electricity. Water from the ocean depths cools these gases once they have been used. This turns them back into liquid to start the process all over again.

▶ Ships with sails controlled by computers save fuel. They take longer to make a voyage, but they can save thousands of tonnes of oil a year.

Looking ahead

What will happen to the world's supply of energy? This question worries many people. Some people are afraid that there will not be enough energy for all our needs in the future. Other people are afraid that the way we burn our fossil fuels such as coal, oil and natural gas, will damage the Earth's atmosphere.

Burning fuels

Burning coal and oil changes the air we breathe. It sends tonnes of **chemicals** into the air each day. Factories sometimes spill out waste chemicals into the rivers or into the air. Traffic also gives off gases which can poison the air. This is called **pollution**. Scientists think that pollution may be the reason why many trees have died in North America and Europe. It may also be the reason why some rivers and lakes have no

fish in them now. Power stations which burn coal, however, are blamed for much of the world's air pollution problem.

The main offenders are the industrial countries. They use most of the world's coal, oil and natural gas. These fossil fuels still supply about 90 per cent of the energy we use. This is **non-renewable** energy.

▲ This wind generator is in Spain. In future, we may see more generators like this all over the world.

◄ In some parts of the world, hot water bubbles to the surface. At this geothermal power station in Australia, the water is used to generate electricity. Scientists are looking for other ways to use the heat inside the Earth.

Pollution will still be a problem when the world's stocks of oil and natural gas have all gone. This is because large stocks of coal are still untouched. More coal will be burned in the future, unless new sources of energy are developed first. When all the coal, as well as the oil and natural gas, has gone, the people of the future will have to use other types of energy. They will have no other choice.

Wasting energy

We waste a great deal of the energy we produce. The demand for more coal, oil and natural gas continues to grow. If only people stopped wasting energy, the demand for fuel would fall.

Huge amounts of heat escape into the atmosphere each year through walls, windows, roofs and chimneys. We throw away many 'waste' products. Some paper, metals and glass can be used again. This is called **recycling**. Furnaces have already been built to burn rubbish to make

electricity. Taking greater care of sources of energy like this is called **conservation**.

Mixed energy

Wind and water power on their own cannot supply all the energy which will be needed in the future. The best use for wind and water power will be to help make the world's supplies of coal, oil and natural gas last longer. The main advantages of wind and water power are that they are renewable. They are also cheap to run and sometimes cheaper to build than other power stations. They do not spoil the air. Wind farms might soon be a familiar sight on hills or at sea. Tidal power stations and wave power stations may be built around the coasts. People will probably have to change the way they live to make more and better use of these types of energy. In future, we will probably see many more ways of using the Sun's energy. Winds, rivers, waves and tides may all help to provide the world with the energy it needs.

In the future the world may use all these different sources of energy.

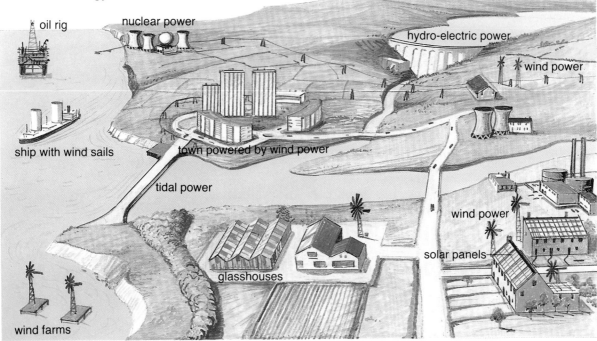

oil rig

nuclear power

hydro-electric power

wind power

ship with wind sails

town powered by wind power

tidal power

wind power

glasshouses

solar panels

wind farms

Glossary

air pressure: the way in which layers of air press down on the Earth. The greatest pressure is felt at ground level. The higher up you go, the less air there is and the lower the air pressure becomes

aqueduct: a channel built to carry water across a valley or through an underground tunnel. The first aqueducts were built by the Romans and were made up of stone or brick

atmosphere: the layer of gases that surround a planet. The Earth's atmosphere is the air. It is made of several gases

barrage: a dam across a river

base load: the lowest amount of electricity that power stations can expect to supply each day throughout the year

breastshot: a mill wheel which is turned by water pushing it in the middle

buttress dam: a type of dam where there is extra strength in the blocks of concrete, or buttresses, built at the front of the dam wall

carbohydrate: an energy-giving substance made by green plants

chemical: any substance which can change when joined or mixed with another substance

compressed air: air squeezed into a container so that its pressure is higher than the air outside

conduct: to guide or channel something along a particular path. Electricity is easily conducted along copper wire

conservation: the protection and careful use of something. The protection of the countryside, wildlife or old buildings is called conservation

electric current: a flow of electricity

electrical energy: a kind of energy or power which can travel along wires. It is used to heat and light homes and to work many machines

electron: a tiny particle of electricity which is found in all atoms. It carries a negative charge

energy: the power to do work. People get energy from food. Engines get energy from fuel like petrol

Equator: an imaginary circle around the middle of the Earth. The hottest parts of the world are nearest to the Equator

estuary: the wide mouth of a river where it meets the sea

evaporate: to change from a liquid into a gas. Heat from the Sun makes water evaporate into the air

force of gravity: the force that pulls everything towards the centre of the Earth. Gravity makes objects fall and gives them weight

fossil fuel: a material that can be burned that comes from the remains of animals and plants which lived millions of years ago. Coal and oil are fossil fuels

generate: to make or create something

generator: a machine for changing mechanical energy into electrical energy

geothermal energy: a type of energy produced by using the heat from below the Earth's surface

head of water: a way of measuring the force of water at a dam or waterfall

headrace: the channel or chute which takes water from a river or lake to a water wheel

high pressure: when air pressure is high, it is greater than normal

horizontal mill: a windmill in which the sails turn around level with, or parallel to, the ground

horsepower: a measurement of power. In the past people compared the power of a machine with the amount of work a single horse could do

hydro-electric power: electricity which has been made by using fast-flowing water to drive a turbine

industry: the work which makes or produces goods, often in a factory

irrigation: watering land that has too little rain by using a system of pipes and ditches. The water is pumped from rivers, lakes or from under the ground. Irrigation makes it possible to grow crops in the desert

kinetic energy: the energy in something when it moves

leat: a channel taking water to a water wheel

low pressure: when air pressure is low, it is lower than normal

magnetism: having the power to attract

mechanical energy: energy which is used to do a job, such as by a person, by a machine, or by an animal

millstone: a flat, round stone used for crushing grain into flour

natural gas: a gas often found close to oil. Most of it is methane gas

non-renewable: something which cannot be replaced

nuclear energy: the power produced by the heat made when atoms are split

ocean current: the steady flow in one direction of a large amount of water in an ocean

overshot: a mill wheel which is turned by water pushing from above

peak load: the highest amount of electricity that power stations have to be able to supply. A peak load happens when there is a sudden demand for power

penstock: the gate or channel controlling a flow of water

Persia: a country now called Iran. It was once an ancient empire which stretched from Egypt to India

pollution: something which dirties or poisons the air, land or water. Wastes from factories cause pollution

post mill: a wooden windmill built on a thick post. The mill could be turned on this post so that the sails could face the wind

potential energy: energy which is stored ready for use at a later time

power line: a wire cable carrying electricity

proton: a tiny particle of electricity which is found in all atoms. It carries a positive charge

pumped storage system: a system of using cheap, plentiful electricity at night, to pump water for a higher level. The water is then re-used to make hydro-electricity during the day when there is a much greater demand for electric power

pylon: a tall steel frame or column for supporting electricity cables above the ground

recycling: to use a waste material again. Paper, metals and glass can all be recycled

renewable: can be replaced, or made new again

reservoir: a very large tank or lake where water is collected and stored

rotation: turning around in a circle or spinning

shaft: a long handle or pole which is used to carry or pull something along. In an engine, a metal rod carries the power from the engine to the wheels

sluice gate: a gate in a waterway which is used to change the flow of water. It can be opened to control the amount of water going through, or closed to hold the water back

smock mill: another name for a tower mill. Only the top of the windmill turns around to face the wind

solar energy: energy from the Sun's rays. Solar energy can be used to make electricity

spillway: a channel taking water away from a dam after it has been used

static electricity: an electric charge produced by rubbing

swell: describes a regular up and down movement of the sea

tailrace: the channel or chute taking water away from a water wheel after it has been used

tower mill: a tall windmill. Only the very top of the windmill turns around to face the wind

transformer: a machine which changes the force of an electric current

troposphere: the layer of air about 12 km thick just above the surface of the Earth. It is named after two Greek words meaning 'movement' (tropos) and 'ball' (sphere). The troposphere is thicker at the Equator than at the two Poles

turbine: a wheel which has many curved blades. It is spun around rapidly by the movement of gas or a liquid. Turbines drive machines which make electricity

undershot: a mill wheel which is turned by water pushing from below

vane: a flat or curved blade. It can be set to direct the flow of air or a liquid, or be free to move to produce power or show a direction

vertical: upright. When people stand up straight, they are in a vertical position

vertical mill: a windmill in which the sails turn around at right angles to the ground

volt: a measurement of the force of an electric current

water cycle: describes the movement of water from the air to the ground and sea and back again to the air

water vapour: water as a gas

weir: a low dam built across a river. Water flows over the top of the weir when the river is full

wind current: a flow of a large amount of air in one direction

Index